My Favorite Fresno County CA Mountain Passes

Acknowledgements

1. S. Madsen for the photographs used in the section on Potter Pass.
2. Sharon Matson for reading the material prior to submission and transportation.
3. Paige Darden representing MyTopo, a Trimble Company for permission to use reproductions of their software maps.

Preface

Often my civilian and clerical lives merge. As a cleric there is a kind of prophetic mindset. By this I don't mean future telling as much as stating reality in a way that uncovers what is obvious. I also don't mean this in a critical sense either because it is often too easy to distort the prophetic role into that of a critic or simply a grumbler. The older we become, the easier it is to do this.

It is obvious to me, that most of the world, including Fresno County California residents, is not aware of the beauty that lies hidden in the mountains and wilderness of Fresno County. Much of this beauty is found along the wilderness trails of eastern Fresno County. We have become a nation that drives to beautiful places. Much of the appeal of Yosemite is the easy access to so much of the beauty that resides there. The places I am referring to are not accessible by automobile.

John Muir understood the importance and the need for humans to spend time in the wilderness. There is a two-fold effect of immersing oneself in the wilderness. We need to be freed from the distractive white noise of civilized living and once again attune to and reacquaint ourselves with the primitive sounds and smells of the wilderness. Once we have 'acclimatized', we have eyes to see and ears to hear once again. We are not blocking things out. We are taking things in.

I wrote this kindle book to share what I have discovered in Fresno County California with those who are not familiar with her rugged beauty. It may seem odd to some that the combination of rock, trees and water can be so varied and wondrously beautiful. The primary purpose of this piece is to pass on beauty that is difficult to access and rarely shared in color. In a digital publication format, Kindle makes this possible. It would be too costly to produce a color version in paperback.

I am thankful that my health and fitness level allow me at the age of sixty nine, to continue to take on the effort required to find and experience the mountain passes that I am sharing. I train daily with the idea in mind to return to the mountains. There is an emotional lift to reaching these high places where most linger to chat with other mountain pilgrims. This work then is both educational and a sharing of the beauty that I have been able to capture in photographs. I hope others will be attracted by the beauty and see first-hand for themselves. I have offered suggested routes which are rough guidelines that are not intended to take the place of detailed maps. A wilderness permit from the agency that controls the entry point is required for all wilderness travel that requires an overnight stay. For those of you who are unable to travel the trails, this is an opportunity to see the beauty from your chair. Someday it will be the same for me.

"The mountains are calling and I must go." John Muir.

Fr. Dale Matson September 2013

Introduction

Mountain Passes and Fresno County California
<u>Fresno County</u>
Wait a minute! I thought Fresno County was known for its agriculture; its fruits and nuts. Well, the western half of the county is known for agriculture. Fresno County is the sixth largest county in California and the forty third largest county in the U.S. with an area of nearly 6,000 square miles. *The Eastern third of Fresno County is wilderness and high Sierras.* Those who backpack here from around the world are aware of this more than most of the half million folks who reside in the city of Fresno.

I have had the privilege of being a civilian on the Fresno County Sherriff's Search and Rescue (SAR) Team for nearly a decade. It has allowed me to travel in and appreciate most of the Fresno County wilderness areas. These areas include the John Muir Wilderness, the Sierra National Forest, Kaiser Wilderness and much of Kings Canyon National Park. There are small herds of Sierra Nevada Bighorn Sheep in Fresno County. They are endangered but making a comeback with human help. I briefly spotted two sheep in Sixty Lakes Basin this summer. The John Muir Trail (JMT) begins in Yosemite Park to the north and runs through the Sierra National Forest and Kings Canyon National Park, both of which are in Fresno County. The third highest mountain in California is in Fresno County. North Palisade is 13,249' and a favorite of mountaineers.

As someone who has been fortunate enough to section hike the John Muir Trail, be flown into other wilderness areas by Eagle One the SAR helicopter, backpack remote areas of Fresno County like the Sixty Lakes Basin and Humphreys' Basin, there is no other area I have visited with any more beauty than Eastern Fresno County.

So, yes the answer is that *Fresno County is known for agriculture and for wilderness activities.* It has more lakes than any other California County. I have always been an out-doorsman and was a member of the forestry club in my high school back in Michigan. I once said to a trail running friend, "I wish I had been born here in California." He responded, "You don't have to be born here but it's important to get here as soon as possible." I agree.

Mountain Passes

Fresno County has over 50 gaps (also known as cols) which are essentially low spots between peaks or low spots on a high ridge. Not all passes have a view. For example, Kaiser Pass has no view and can be driven over by car. Mountain peaks and passes have one major thing in common. They provide a unique perspective; a singular view. Peak bagging has a singular mission to reach the top. I have done some peak bagging but the peaks are what can be termed *"walk ups"*. There are no mountaineering skills required. Being an average person, walk up peaks like Kaiser, Half Dome, Cloud's Rest, Mitchell, Alta, Givens, Hoffman and even Mt. Whitney have been accomplished as day hikes.

Mountain passes are different than peaks because they are traversed as a means to get to another place. It also means that the pass can be approached from more than one direction. For example, most of the passes on the JMT can be crossed from south to north or north to south. In fact, mountain passes can actually be higher than many mountain peaks. Glenn Pass (11,978') is higher than Kaiser Peak (10,320'). Passes are high altitude 'assurance markers'. They help us orient. Often there is a sign denoting the pass name and altitude. Passes are also used as boundaries between counties or parks. Kearsarge Pass (11,760') is an east-west boundary between Inyo and Fresno Counties. Forester Pass

(13,200') is a boundary between Kings Canyon to the north and Sequoia National Park to the south.

This is about mountain passes but it is also about a portion of Fresno County of which even residents are generally unaware. I am an adopted son of Fresno County having lived here only my last twenty two years. Those years have been filled with personal growth and a spiritual joy that is enhanced by being in the mountains. Is it any wonder that the Israelites received God's words from the mountains in the wilderness?

Mountain Passes

Potter Pass
Silver and Goodale Passes
Selden Pass
Muir Mather and Pinchot
Kearsarge and Glen Passes
Piute Pass

Potter Pass

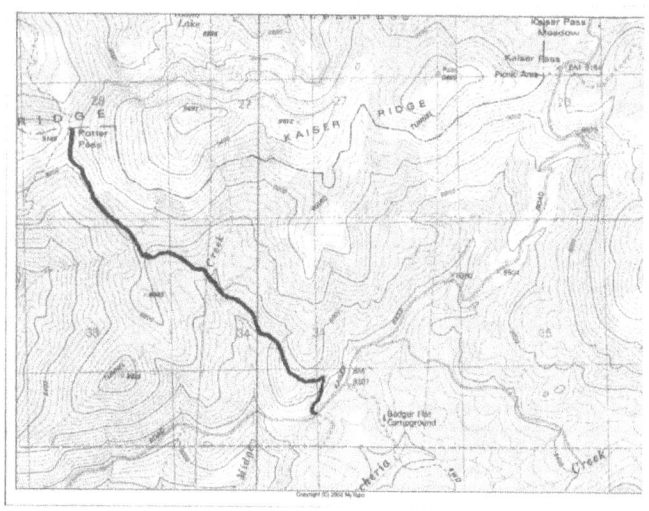

Elevation: 8,980'
Location: 37 17' 14.5" N 119 08' 23" W
Trailhead Distance from Fresno: 3.0 hours
Distance to pass from trailhead: 2.2 miles
Elevation gain: 680'
Degree of difficulty   hiker must be fit and sound
Directions to trailhead: From   Fresno,
take Highway 168 east to Kaiser Pass Road (near Hunting-
ton Lake). Turn right on Kaiser Pass Road and drive about
20 minutes to the Badger Flat parking area on right. There is
a potty by the parking. The trailhead is on the other side of
the road.

For those who live in Fresno, the closest pass with
a view is Potter Pass. There are two access points off Kaiser
Pass Road. The trail out of Badger Flat has less altitude gain.
When hiking, I either like to hike to a view or to water. The

Potter Pass trail can provide both if you go beyond the pass to Twin Lakes and further to George Lake. There is also a variety of wildflowers along the trail. After Potter Pass, Twin lakes are about 1.5 miles further and George Lake is an additional mile with a climb to about 9,100'. I think the view at George Lake is worth the extra effort. You can see Kaiser Peak (10,310) above from George Lake.

Lower Twin Lake

Upper Twin Lake

George Lake

While there is no view to the south, the pass itself provides a wonderful and unobstructed view to the north for a distance of about 30 miles. In the view, you may be surprised to see the Ritter Range including Banner Peak and Mt. Ritter.

Mt. Ritter and Banner Peak

Also, don't be surprised to see cattle grazing in the meadow below Potter Pass. My wife Sharon likes to swim to the island in Upper Twin Lake.

Tom Harrison Maps recently (2013) published a map of the "Kaiser Wilderness" which is quite helpful and provides distances at trail junctions. One can hike to the pass and head back to the trailhead or go all the way to George Lake depending on one's ability and fitness. If you resupply your water in the lakes, have a means to purify it with you.

Silver and Goodale Passes

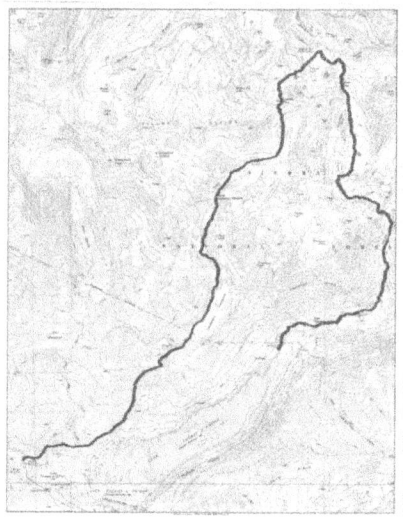

Elevation: 10,719' Silver 10,991' Goodale
Location: 37 28' 4" N 118 55' 19 W (Silver)
Location: 37 27' 48" N 118 56' 22" W
Trailhead Distance from Fresno: 3.5 hours
Distance to pass from trailhead: 9 miles (Silver)
Elevation gain: 3,325'
Degree of difficulty *extremely difficult* day hike. The 21 mile counterclockwise loop can also be done as an overnight, staying at one of the lakes. See map.

Directions to trailhead: From Fresno, take Highway 168 east to Kaiser Pass Road (near Huntington Lake). Turn right on Kaiser Pass Road drive over Kaiser Pass to the fork in the road. Take the left hand fork 7 more miles to Edison Lake. **Caution** the last 14 miles is a one lane road best traversed with a four wheel drive or a high clearance vehicle. It will take an hour to go 14 miles!

The first run of the Edison Lake water taxi out of

Vermilion Valley Resort (see information on the website) to the east end of the lake is usually about 9am. Earlier departures can be arranged for an additional fee. I also recommend this trip be done when the lake is high and the ferry can drop you off close to the trail that connects with the (northbound) John Muir trail junction. I have been dropped off at least a mile further away when the water is low. Be careful not to head south toward Selden Pass.

Edison Lake Water Taxi

Last year (2012) I did the 21 mile loop in a single day but arranged for a 7:30 am departure to the east end of the lake. I finished by about 5pm and drove back to Fresno. Unless you are "marathon fit", I would recommend an overnight at one of the lakes near Silver Pass. I was only carrying about five pounds of food and gear including a map and GPS. climbing two passes in a single day can be a challenge but both offer stunning views. After going over Silver Pass, be careful to notice when the JMT and Goodale Pass trails part. The JMT continues north and the Goodale Pass trail heads southwest. If you only want to hike to Silver Pass as an out and back, keep an eye on your watch. Your return time will be about the same as your outbound time, in order to catch the last run of the water taxi.

Silver Lake below Silver Pass

View South from Silver Pass

View North from Silver Pass

Lake of the Lone Indian

Goodale Pass view

Goodale Pass view two

Continuing the loop beyond Goodale Pass

Selden Pass

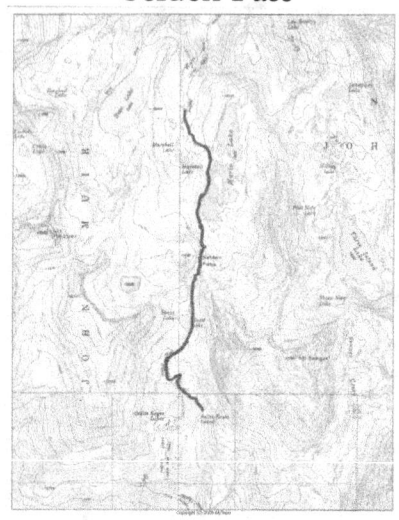

Elevation: 10,900'
Location: 37 17' 23" N 118 52' 19" W
Trailhead Distance from Fresno: 3.5 hours
Distance trailhead to pass: 10.5 miles
Elevation gain: *3,400'* (plenty of climb)
Degree of difficulty   this requires an overnight at Sallie Keys Lake or Heart Lake

Directions to trailhead: F r o m Fresno, take Highway 168 east to Kaiser Pass Road (near Huntington Lake). Turn right on Kaiser Pass Road and continue over Kaiser Pass on a one land road to the fork in the road. Take the right fork 7 more miles to Florence Lake. Take the first water taxi (check schedule on web but it is usually 8:30am) to the southeast end of the lake and climb up to the trailhead.

Hike toward Kings Canyon but just east of Muir Camp, there is a sign to head north to Selden Pass. This trail eventually hits the JMT as it climbs north. Be on the lookout for rattle snakes on the trail out of Florence Lake. The climb out of the Muir Camp area is exposed, steep, long and hot. Have lots of water since there is none until you cross *Senger Creek.*

A friend and I did this a few years back. We hiked to the Sallie Keys Lakes and made camp There are several nice established campsites near the lakes. We then hiked up to the pass with just a water bottle. The view is great in both directions. If the intent is to return to the ferry landing the following day, don't expect it to be any faster inbound than it was outbound. The ferry runs every two hours. There is a phone in a shack to let the taxi know you need to be picked up.

Selden Pass Sign near Muir Camp

Sallie Keys Lake

Heart Lake

Looking South from Selden Pass

Marie Lake North of Selden Pass

Muir Mather and Pinchot Passes

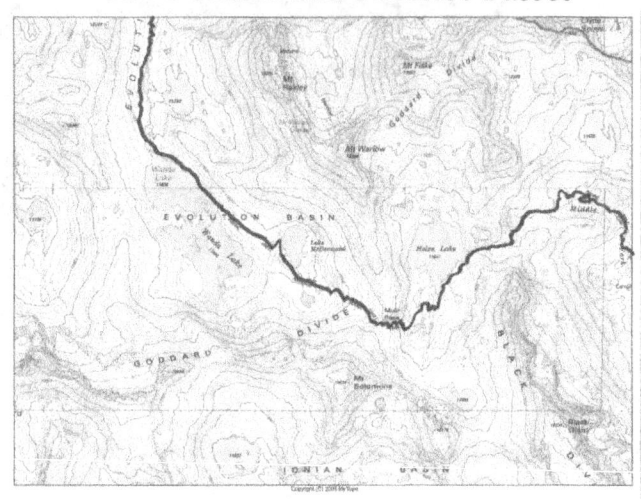

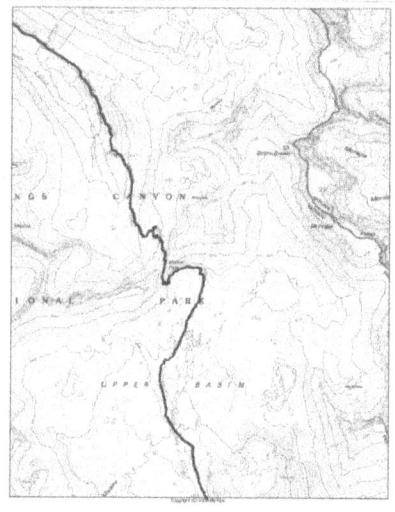

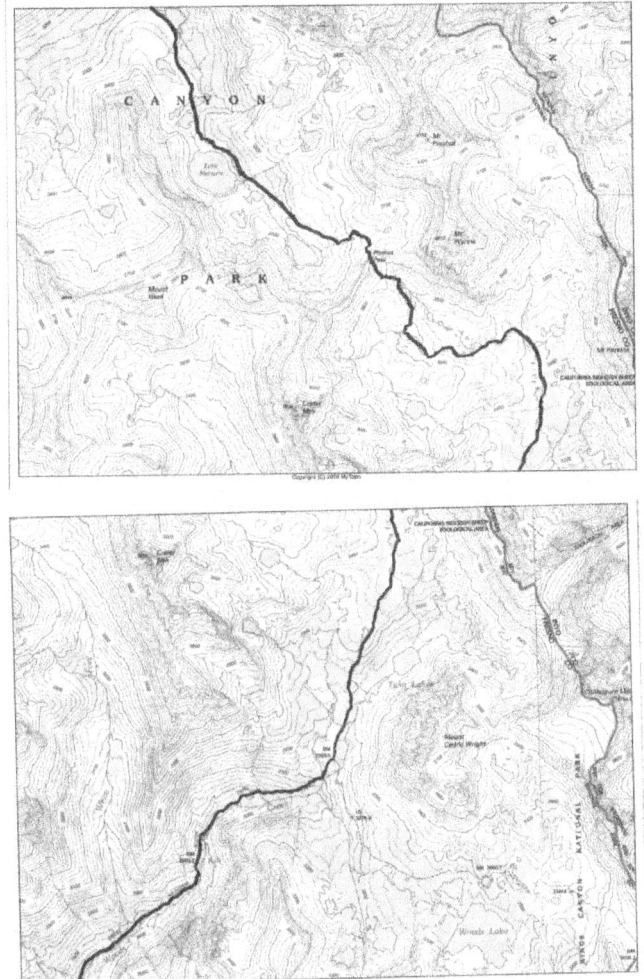

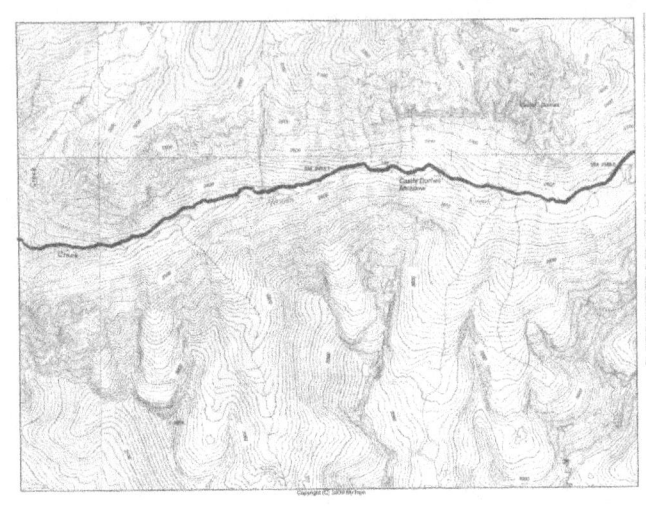

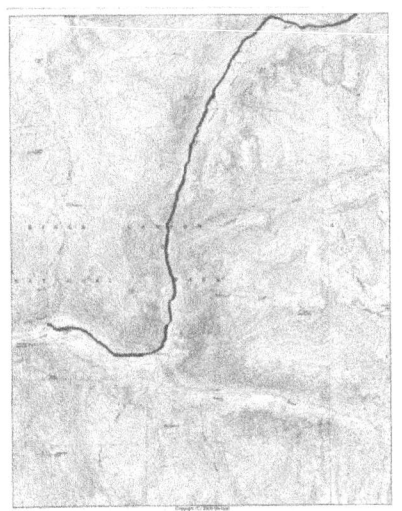

| Elevation: | 11,955' Muir   12,100' Mather |
| Elevation | 12,130' Pinchot |

Location:	37 6' 44" N 118 40' 11" W	Muir
Location:	37 01' 53 N 118 27' 32" W	Mather
Location:	36 56' 11" N 118 24' 42" W	P i n -

chot

Trailhead Distance from Fresno: 3.5 hours

Distance to pass from trailhead: 2   6
miles (SE end Florence Lake to Muir Pass)
Elevation gain: 11,713'
for entire the ***81 mile point to point hike***
Degree of difficulty   *difficult*
Directions to trailhead: From   Fresno,
take Highway 168 east to Kaiser Pass Road (near Huntington Lake). Turn right on Kaiser Pass Road drive over Kaiser
Pass (the road becomes one lane) to the fork in the road.
Take the right fork 7 more miles to Florence Lake. Take
the first water taxi (check schedule on web but it is usually
8:30am) to the southeast end of the lake and climb up to the
trailhead.

      This is my all-time favorite solo hike done in 2012. I
did a YouTube video of it called "The Heart of the John Muir
Trail." It required my wife Sharon dropping me off at Florence Lake and picking me up at Roads End in Cedar Grove
in Kings Canyon National park. She hiked in and met me
just below the Mist Falls on the Woods Creek trail. I was
more than ready to see her again.

      The hike, beginning at the southeast end of Florence
Lake, joins the JMT shortly before the trail enters Kings
Canyon National Park. As you cross the bridge over Piute
Creek, you are immediately met with a view of Pavilion
Dome (11, 856'). At this point, you are 9 miles from Flor-
ence Lake and a long way from anywhere else. Personally,
I believe because of the difficulty reaching this area, it has
remained some of the most pristine wilderness in the U.S.

      I had hiked this section twice before, headed to Mc-
Clure Meadow with family and friends. Both times we had
stopped along a wooded section of the San Joaquin River
for the night and then camped the following night near the
ranger station in McClure Meadow. The meadow has one of
the most stunning views I have ever seen with the mountains
as a backdrop for Evolution Creek. In 2012, I had a pack

that weighed only 25 pounds (including bear canister) and was traveling at the fast pace of two miles per hour. On the first day, I made it all the way to Evolution Lake which is dominated on the south end by Mt. Spencer (12,431). The beauty of the area continues to expand and overwhelms you the further down the trail you go.

Wanda Lake

When you arrive at Wanda Lake (named after one of Muir's daughters), you can see the Muir Hut at Muir Pass in the distance with the naked eye. It doesn't seem too far but it is. I arrived at Muir Pass about 8:30am on day two. The hut was constructed as a memorial to Muir but intended only for emergency use.

Muir Hut

Muir Pass Looking North

Muir Pass looking south

Black Giant

This pass has been known to have snow even in summer some years. The lake to the south is Helen Lake, named after Muir's other daughter. It is an absolute pearl with Mt. Warlow (13,212') pictured in the background.

Helen Lake

The descent from Muir Pass into Le Conte Canyon seems never-ending and steep. The JMT elevation near the ranger station is 8,750', a drop of over 3,200' at that point and elevation that will have to be recaptured climbing up the Golden Staircase to Mather Pass. This was one of the later parts of the JMT to be completed and required extensive blasting. I stayed in at a small campsite in Deer Meadow my second night. It rained during the night and the air was fresh and clear the next morning as I began to climb the Golden Staircase. There was an incredible moment as the trail climbed along Palisade Creek and the rain induced, fog shrouded, Palisades came into view.

Palisades in fog

There are "fourteeners" in this group including North Palisade in Fresno County. It is the 3rd highest peak in the Sierras (14,249'). By the time you get to the 2nd Palisades Lake, the trail is well above it. The pass was named after Stephen Mather head of the U.S. Park Service and Assistant Secretary of the Interior. It is a grand view looking back to the north and looking south toward Pinchot Pass.

Lower Palisades Lake

Looking North from Mather Pass

Looking South from Mather Pass

South Fork of the Kings River

Pinchot Pass was named after Gifford Pinchot who was the first head of the U.S. Forest Service and the 28th Governor of Pennsylvania.

By the time the trail crosses over the South Fork of the Kings River, the altitude is down to 10,000' and one must immediately begin reclaiming the loss as one climbs toward Pinchot Pass.

Marjorie Lake

View North from Pinchot Pass of Marjorie Lake
and a small unnamed lake above it

Human-like Head on mountain at Pinchot Pass

The weather became sketchy again with intermittent rain and thunder. I decided to push on and passed beautiful Marjorie Lake. There is a smaller unnamed lake above it as you climb toward the pass. I reached Pinchot Pass at 5:45pm the third day and called Sharon on my satellite phone to let her know about where I would be staying the night on the south side of the pass. I was hoping to get to Twin Lakes. It began to rain again and get dark. I was tired and decided to camp near a small unnamed lake in some scrub evergreen. I needed my headlight as I finished setting up my tent. Sierra Nevada Bighorn Sheep have been sighted around Pinchot Pass so keep a watchful eye.

The following morning I hiked down to the junction of the Woods Creek Trail and headed out the final 15 miles to Roads End. This was truly the heart of the John Muir Trail.

Woods Creek headed toward Roads End

Castle Domes
Kearsarge and Glen Passes

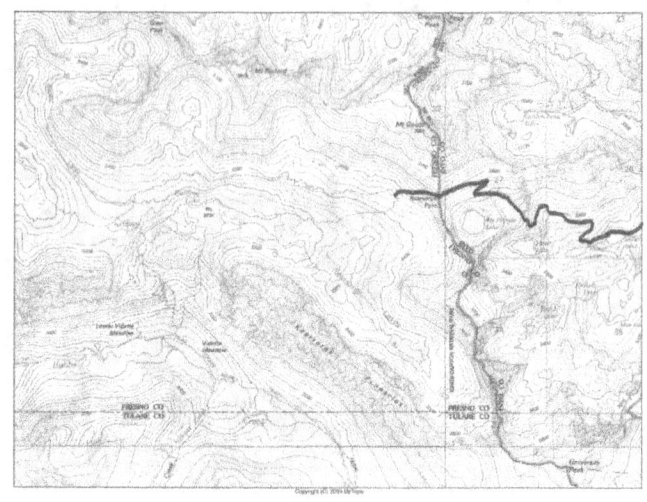

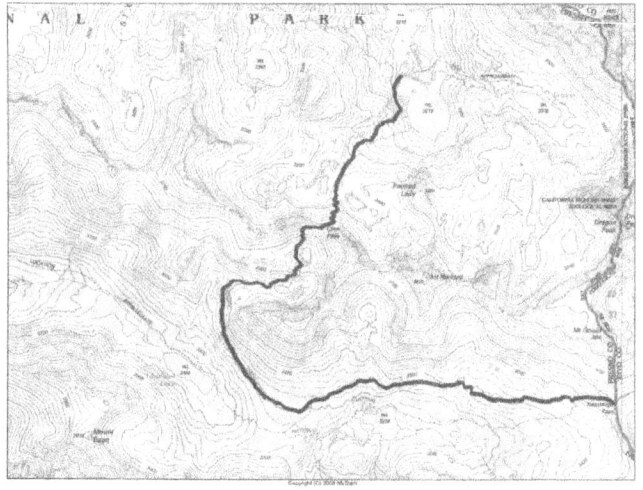

Elevation: 11,760' Kearsarge
Elevation: 11,978' Glen Pass
Location: 36 46' 24" N 118 22' 33" W Kearsarge
Location: 36 47' 22" N 118 24' 39" W Glen
        Trailhead Distance from Fresno: 5 hours to
Onion Valley Trailhead
        Distance from trailhead to pass: 5.5miles

(Kearsarge)
Distance from trailhead to pass: 12miles (Glen)
   Elevation gain: 4,200'
(Onion Valley to Glen Pass
Degree of difficulty Extreme as day hike

Directions to trailhead: From Fresno, take Highway 99 South to Bakersfield and the 198 exit East toward Barstow. Then take Highway 14 North to Highway 395 North. Pick up your wilderness permit in Lone Pine after 8am or after 11am of the previous day and head north to Independence. Turn left at the post office and head west to the trailhead (9,200) at Onion Valley. (I find this is faster than taking highway 120 through Yosemite and heading south.) It is also faster than coming in from Road's End in Cedar Grove on the west side where the hike is over 21 miles and 7,000' of altitude gain from the trailhead at Road's End.

  The name Kearsarge was taken from the name of a mine on the east side of the pass. This hike actually starts in the Inyo Nation Forest. (this why you will get the permit in Inyo County). The climb up to Kearsarge is steep but the trail is good. Purify the water you use to resupply with along the way. You will pass a couple creeks and pass near one of the lakes for resupply but have extra water when you hit the pass. This is a well-traveled trail.

  When you reach the pass, you will lose sight of the Inyo County lakes except for Big Pothole Lake behind you.

Big Pothole Lake

You will see the vast expanse of the Owens Valley. The pass is a boundary between Inyo and Fresno Counties. The west side is also Kings Canyon National Park. To the west, the view is simply amazing.

Below Kearsarge Pass Looking East

Kearsarge Pass Looking West

Kearsarge Pinnacles

Mt. Gould (12,012') immediately above Kearsarge Pass

Author at Kearsarge Pass

Some of the prominent features are the Kearsarge Pinnacles, Kearsarge Lakes at their base and Bullfrog Lake. While fairly near, Glen Pass is hidden to the north. The high trail heads to Glen Pass and Rae Lakes. It is a fairly flat trail until the climb to Glen Pass which was named for Glen Crow.

Unique shape of Charlotte Dome

Charlotte Lake from trail above

The climb begins at a point above Charlotte Lake below on the left. (Seasoned Ranger Rick Sanger is stationed there). I'm not sure why but Glen Pass has always been a slow climb for me northbound. I have to takes breaks about every other switchback toward the end.

Small unnamed lake below trail to Glen Pass

Glen Pass South

Glen Pass North toward Rae Lakes

Those who are cautious about edges will not be comfortable until you drop down a bit on the other side of the pass. Glen Pass is one of my favorite views with Rae Lakes to the North and a host of peaks to the south including East Vidette Peak (12,356') and Mt. Brewer (13.576') to the south.

By this time for me, it was getting well into the afternoon and I was happy to descend to Rae Lakes and look for a campsite.

Painted Lady

Fin Dome

(There is also a backcountry ranger stationed at Rae Lakes) the two most prominent features at Rae Lakes are Fin Dome and the Painted Lady.

There is a special note at this point. Sierra Nevada Bighorn Sheep have been sighted along much of this route at times including the Rae Lakes area.

Piute Pass

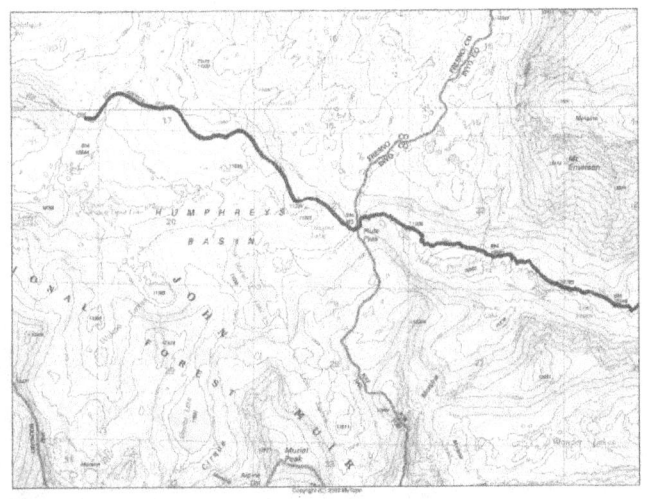

Elevation: 11,408'
Location: 37 14' 20.5 N 118 40' 60" W
Trailhead Distance from Fresno: 5.5 hours
Distance from trailhead to pass: 6 miles
Elevation gain: 2,052'
Degree of difficulty   hiker must be fit and sound

Directions to trailhead: From Fresno, take Highway 41 north to Yosemite. Take 120 (Tioga Pass Road) east to Highway 395. Head south to Bishop and pick up the trail permit there (Inyo County entry point). Take the road "Line Road" or Highway 168 east to the North Lake road and the North Lake trailhead near the pack station. Walk a half mile to the trailhead (9,356') to Piute Pass. Earlier in the year, I attempted this as an overnight from the west side at Florence Lake. After hiking 20 miles I was still 2 miles from Piute Pass heading east and camped about a mile west of where we stayed coming in from the east. It is simply less difficult to come from the east side.

This hike begins in Inyo County and Piute Pass (named after the local Piute Indians) is the boundary between Inyo and Fresno Counties. This hike was a return of sorts for me since I was dropped off by helicopter about seven years ago about a mile west of the pass. I was part of the Fresno County Search and Rescue Team (SART) looking for a lost hiker. As I looked around I couldn't believe how beautiful it was. It was gradually dawning on me that Fresno County while unknown by most was every bit as beautiful as Yosemite where I had spent so many hours.

Piute Lake

Final view to East before Pass

When you reach Piute Pass, the view is rather expansive and beautiful. The surrounding basin (Humphrys') is above 11,000' so there are few trees. The trail west splits with the southern part heading to Muriel Lake.

Piute Pass looking west to Summit Lake

Looking west to Pinnacles

My wife Sharon enjoying the view
We headed toward the northern shore above
Summit Lake where we set up our tent and stowed
our gear before heading toward Desolation Lake.

Piute Pass looking back from campsite

The 'use trail' off the Piute Creek trail leading northwest takes you first to Lower Desolation Lake and then to Desolation Lake. It is obvious why both are called "Desolation" because of the lack of anything other than rocks and water. They are beautiful nonetheless. Pilot Knob can also be seen near Desolation Lake.

Desolation Lake with Pilot Knob on left

The most prominent feature is Mt. Humphreys just shy of 14,000'. It is singular and beautiful.

This area begs for further exploration further west on the Piute Creek Trail and the north into French Basin on the Pine Creek trail.

Mountains

Fr. Dale Matson

"Great is the LORD, and highly to be praised,
And His greatness is unsearchable.
One generation shall praise Your works to another,
And shall declare Your mighty acts.
On the glorious splendor of Your majesty
And on Your wonderful works, I will meditate.
Men shall speak of the power of Your awesome acts,
And I will tell of Your greatness.
They shall eagerly utter the memory of Your abundant
goodness
And will shout joyfully of Your righteousness." (Psalm 145:
3-7)

Mountains are frequently associated with God in the Holy Scriptures. Often it is a pivotal time in the history of God's people. Noah's Ark came to rest on *Mount Ararat.* Abraham took his son Isaac to *Mount Moriah* intending to sacrifice him. *Mt Moriah* is also the site of Solomon's Temple. *Mt Sinai* (Horeb) was where God revealed Himself to Moses and where the Ten Commandments were given. It was *Mount Nebo* where Moses struck the rock to provide water. It was *Mount Zion* where David built his palace and it was the *Mount of Olives* where Jesus delivered His sermon and where He was arrested. *Mount Tabor* is traditionally understood to be the place of His transfiguration. Even one of God's names, El Shaddai can be translated "God of the Mountain" (NJB).

I was born and raised in Michigan where my family also visited the Porcupine Mountains near Lake Superior in the Upper Peninsula. As a child they seemed imposing at about 1,600' of elevation. In the mid 1960's a friend of mine Dan McCosh and I drove to California from Michigan in June and I saw mountains, real mountains, for the first time. As we approached Loveland Colorado, The Rockies emerged immediately and abruptly from the plains. My heart nearly stopped as we anticipated driving over Loveland Pass at nearly 12,000', my hands immediately began to sweat. There was still considerable snow along the sides of the road as we crossed the Continental Divide. This view of the Rocky Mountains approaching Loveland made such an indelible impression on me that I knew someday I would live in an area where I could view and travel in God's glorious mountains.

Now, in my twentieth year in Fresno CA, when the air is clear I can see much of the central Sierra Nevada Mountains. The mountains offer year round recreation and I am there once a week. There is no way to describe how my spirit is elevated each time I drive east into the mountains to begin a new adventure with friends or in the company of my Airedales Susie and Duke who change from pets to companions who especially enjoy the winter snow. I also spent four of the best days of my life with my sons as we backpacked a portion of the John Muir Trail together. Hearing them talking together as men around a campfire as I fell asleep in my tent was as beautiful a sound as any waterfall or river.

These mountain places are where I fellowship with God too for it was He who made these things and us also. It can at times be as intimate an occasion for me as when I proclaim the words of the Great Thanksgiving during the Holy Eucharist.

Climb the mountains and get their good tidings. Nature's peace will flow into you as sunshine flows into trees. The winds will blow their own freshness into you, and the storms their energy, while cares will drop off like autumn leaves. ~John Muir